THE LONESOME BEAUTY OF THE MOMENT

Also by Lee Bassett

Unknown Tongues 1973
The Mapmaker's Lost Daughter 1980
Hatsutaiken 1980
Gauguin and Food 1982
News from the Past Mistakes Hermitage 1983
Lucy and the Blue Quail 1985

The Lonesome Beauty of the Moment

Poems by Lee Bassett

Photographs by Jake Seniuk

Blue Begonia Press

The Lonesome Beauty of the Moment

Poems by Lee Bassett

Photographs by Jake Seniuk

Blue Begonia Press

Many thanks to Jake Seniuk for invaluable work on this book, including inspiration and design. Also, a hearty thanks to those who appeared in the photographs including Frank Jones, Erin McClelland, Scott Moorehead and Lisa Peterson. And thanks to those who assisted in the photographic shoots including Jeff Carter, Mandy Comstock, Miriam Dyak, Susan Seniuk, and Barbara Slavik. And another kind of thank you goes out to Lex Runciman and Liza von Rosenstiel for their steadfast encouragement.

Copyright © 1991 by Lee Bassett
Photographs copyright © 1991 by Jake Seniuk
All Rights Reserved

First Edition

ISBN 0-911287-14-0

Published by
    Blue Begonia Press
    225 South 15th
    Yakima, WA 98902

For Walker Lee and Maddy Blue

*It ain't the getting and spending that wears you out,
it's the toll that hope takes.*

— Stanley Elkin

*I would shut the whole if I could out of harm's way,
As one shuts a holiday photo away in a desk,
Or shuts one's eyes.*

— Bernard Spencer

Contents

The Fourth of July	13
Listen, Josephine	23
In a Darkroom	37
Illicit Love	47
Your Black Crow	59
Afterword	69

The Fourth of July

I

After the war, the blasted out buildings, the broken
Crater-roads, the encampments and harbors and dust.
Men hobbled home and hunched, with hands larger
Than their faces, and women, after all fatigue...
World-weary, world-weary.

After the chaos and war which enthralled us,
The promise and beginnings of prosperous flowers,
The slow endless composition of order and occupation,
And once again, the desire to be imperishable.
After the war, another kind of war.

II

In a park, on the Fourth of July, itinerant jazz-scent
Of magnolia, the bright hot light of the noon-day sun.
A boy, far too big, grinds on the large and loving
Hips of his mother, who holds him.

A long time ago, this fat blazing boy
Slammed from her in a river of pain,
And still she remembers every moment
Of his coming forth, his calling her,
From the darkroom.

III

And suddenly it occurs to her, in a shriek of pride,
His name will be pulled from a jar, called out again,
And he will be ready for war. Wave good-bye,
Down rubs the dirt, wave out to sea, down grinds
The rock. Wave good-bye.

This is how, at times, a pigeon in a park
Will swallow anything, even shards of junk,
Then look up surprised.

IV

Only one moment, between one moment
Of destruction, and the next. Only once.

This is the springing-forth image of you, that day,
On the way to the fireworks, when we missed
The multiple car-crash only by a moment,
When you said that desires were the flares
Of homeless people, lost on the freeway,
When your lost lover flashed up
Like a shadow on your hand,
And the pagan, inscrutable tarantula
And your desire to follow it,
Were the same thing.
To be bitten only once.

V

At dusk, the Northern Bear wakes up in the sky.
She emerges from the dark womb of cave and time,
To enjoy the lightning of the fireworks.
The holy Northern Bear wakes up,
Aching for a fish or a young man.

The sluggish heart of bear begins a dream in men
Who also feel a passion for the light. Men rise up
To women in summer, with a sharp suffering
In their being.

VI

Something deep and wild inside your being
Cries out, and flashes up,
As it must have for Daguerre
And William Fox Talbot, who both
Claimed light on a copper plate as their own,

Who both fought across the water
For this old, old invention,
To own what is lost.

Listen, Josephine

I

The moon is a traveller, its smooth restless face
Moves low among the shelters for the poor
And slowly up to rub the granite tip
Of our tallest building.

And then out among the hills.
On one hill, above the bright dirt-clearing
Where the enemy loaded our horses
And took them away, my gray stone
Waits in the moonlight.
The gift you give, is desire never finished.

II

In the primal lump of night, my chemical white bones
Slip out of the earth, and walk through the fields
Of Wait-A-Bit and Stickseed, who also feel the need
To travel.

Later, I drip from my bath in a lake, and return
To the hole. Down grinds the rock, down rubs the dirt.
Someone dropped photographic plates on my grave.
And the travelling moon shot its light through them,
Shot green pictures on my headstone.

III

Camera Obscura, resin of nitrate, dark chamber.
In the terror of a darkroom, bitumen of Judea,
The intensity of hope and light,
Chloride and bromide.

In the terror of the darkroom,
The unrepeatable moment,
And dark erotic imprint,
A hand embedded on another hand.
Was it you, dark copper flower,
With the crisis-blue eyes?

IV

Listen, Josephine, long before Jesus
Shoved coins off a table in disgust,
And shoved the whole table into the dirt,
A young monk wandered
The green hills of Japan
And discovered suffering.

And it was in the Springtime.
Dark tulips and Wake-Robin, and desire
Always blooms without permission.
As when Bessie Smith,
Chanting like a blue frog in a restless pond,
Climbed all the way up the cold hospital steps,
And it was Spring.

V

And after, the world again, and the war.
A drive to work on the stupid highway of commerce,
A pile of pictures of the brave mountain I never climbed.

And after, the world again, and every now and again,
I am stuck deep in the mud of a remote woods,
And I hear the sharp ring of a telephone.

Or, on private nights, when I cannot forgive myself,
I look up and see a goose fly over,
And she is on fire.
The fire of fidelity.

VI

In a motel, in the huge loneliness of a harsh dark room,
I hear two gods next door, shout and roar in love-making.
Snow outside, the last snow, tiny flakes smaller than dust
Or sand, as if it might be snowing outside,
Or not snowing.

And beyond, snow geese groan low over Main Street,
Temporarily confused in the crazy street lights.
And yet, somehow, they honk their way out,
Asymmetrical,
Magnetic,
Like brothers and sisters.

VII

Sometimes, there are times when I cannot bear
To be alone. Sometimes, I wish that my basic pain
Could melt into the sadness of another.

Sometimes, I wish that when I light a cigar,
My whole body would catch flame.

Sometimes, as if bonding is an emergency,
I turn into someone else
And knock uninvited
On a door.

VIII

And with a hint of what your nakedness might offer,
You came down tonight
To save another human being.
And after, like the migratory wings
That swarmed in to eat the berry-tree,
You moved on.

Here is what happens, when the heart wakes up:
On Halloween, according to the law of sadness,
A man-child comes to our door in costume,
And makes us cry.
And, according to the law of joy,
We open that door,
And a great wind
Full of snow
Turns us.

IX

Under snow-stars, I take the cut of the road
Up a hill to the monastery,
And the sumac-wind carries my body
Up to the bonfire. I watch the big bonfire
Pour sparks
On the glad hearts of monks.

It is Spring, and like Halloween,
The heart wakes up,
The homeless climb up their festive ladders,
And migrant workers follow the harvest here,
To a dark picnic.
It is Spring, and a drowned sailor
Wakes up to play saxophone.

X

Listen, Josephine, you once stopped the car
And pulled over, and saved the tarantula
From the highway.

Another time, you gathered the fragments,
The crushed shells of legs off the highway,
And turned them inside out,
And put them in your hair.

In one privileged moment of lightning,
Your head became a box of light,
And therefore, no self at all,
And it was in the Spring.

In a Darkroom

I

Crowded street, secret meeting, one train ticket.
My hands fly in the mad language against your leaving,
In the fierceness and jazz of the passing moment.
The hot skin of the image stands here before me,
As you were, the one night we had together
In the abandoned house.

The animal-red of war, flushed on the wall.
We saw the crackle of pine-hungry flames, high above
The poor-dirt family who lived there, and the eight or nine
Children who lived there. They will always be remembered,
Their dirty faces, their ten-thousand tiny jumping feet,
All flame, all gone now, all gone, all black
In what becomes the new snow of the morning.

II

This town, our town, still occupied. We only appeared
To each other, on the surface of our bodies.
I remember the blockades, and the fourth night of curfew.
We slipped by the soldiers and scurried down the alley
With the beautiful mouth of stars.

We went down a dark, illegal alley and kissed,
And I remember your hands. We held the globe of each other
And kissed, as stars wedged down between buildings,
As we unraveled centuries of clothing.
You smelled like tarantula.
You tasted like monk's bread.

III

Once, in dark time, snow falling on the town square,
Snow a madness, half-falling
On the picture-taking brain, falling
On the motorcycles of the military police,
I look down deep into my portable image-box
And see the green of a woman in a summer dress,
Snow falling on her bare legs.

Then I raised my head up into the real night.
I hear the wind pound hell into the winter wheat,
And I see a red-bird hammer an enormous hawk.
Far off, I saw a house explode, and closer,

I saw the terror on the face of a man
Who must leave his family.
I saw one tennis shoe, frozen homeless
By the side of the road, no snow,
No wet legs, no girl in a green dress.

IV

Another and another bucket, and I have always
Carried this thin photograph of you,
Embracing a soldier.

A secret house, the fluid and voltage
From room to room, the loosening
Of your fire-damp clothes behind you.
It's as if you will not relax, when he kisses you,
The kiss cannot go inside.

V

And the love-making isn't long enough
Before he goes to sleep, and the shine in the morning
Isn't bright enough, before he goes to work,
And the kiss isn't long enough, before it turns to logic.

Another and another vain-filling of the bucket,
And always the decision, to expose or hide
The rare moment which glows out of time,
And then the glow is gone. Down rubs the dirt,
Down grinds the rock.

VI

The quick soldier's kiss means shame,
And shame means fire. And fire means
Not letting anyone know you.

Another bucket, and across town,
Daguerre's famous diorama blows up in flames.
Houses burn, playgrounds, whole towns.
And even as we speak, the soldiers load
Their useless pails of water in terror and panic,
The water in the buckets
Too hot to hold.

Illicit Love

I

Today, the yellow maple leaves
Shatter bright across my face,
And the fragility of the park
Is beautiful. For today, I saw
A young woman in a green dress,
Shy and uncertain,
Trapped in the back of a family car.

Bored, she bounces her hips
To music which blazes eternal,
And wishes to be looked at,
Or touched perhaps,
Or at least flowing out of the car
Somewhere else.

II

She points her camera at a featureless jogger,
The lazy droop of men playing chess,
The unreadable flat wind.

Next to her in the car is a recent snapshot of herself.
In a moment, a brilliant hawk
Will stare at her body from a tree,
And she will feel the need to grab the photograph,
To see what the hawk sees.
Something quite shattering, like a promised land,
Is about to happen.

III

What is this war, this outsidership, which is also
A promise? What is this here-and-gone song
I especially love to hear, in March,
When the earth begins repairing itself,
When a ditch by the side of the road
Begins to fidget with dark green itch?

I could ask Shelley, whose heart still scrapes
Against the starfish near Portofino.

IV

Or I could ask a saint, like Caterina,
Who exchanged her heart with a living god.
Or I could ask the white moth, who flies
Loosely from the heart of all dead soldiers
Who have no family.

Or I could ask the boy, who is bored
With the adult necessity of waiting for trains,
Why he, by some necessity of his own,
Suddenly bursts into song.

V

Listen, stranger, long before Jesus
Came out of the ground
And saw his own shadow flashed
Permanently on a Hiroshima wall,
A homeless monk wandered the hills
Of Japan, and sang a song of death.

Down rubs the dirt, down grinds the rock,
And suddenly, a mockingbird is shattered
In the woods.
The mockingbird follows a few city mourners
To this hole on the edge
Of the earth.

VI

Above, the last of this year's monstrous snowflakes,
And below, in the mud, a loud gasp
From the trapped shoes.

The soldiers look on, and think I am dead in the box.
But you...you come visit, and lie down beside me illicitly,
And you sing and sing,
Like a cricket caught inside a drawer
Of old photographs,
Like the big beatific blue moan
Of Billie Holiday.

VII

Deep below the rib-rattle,
Your long gypsy hands,
And their great teachings.
Your hands came down like Succubus,
Taking her wet clothes off and mounting me,
While I slept under Heaven.

They were the first to enhance my dumb body,
In one privileged moment,
Saying come to me,
Come to me,
Before the moment is gone.

VIII

Come to me, come bonfire, come hot,
The way a tarantula soaks up the day-heat,
And stores it horizontally,
And radiates it up later,
In the frozen mud night.

Deep below the deep-blue growl
You rumble your come-cry. Come warm in the mud,
Come warm, like the seventh planet from the sun.
Come hot, the way a salamander
Wriggles her succulent hips,
When in revelation,
A rock is overturned.

Your Black Crow

I

And after, the world again,
And a table somewhere,
With bright new holy flowers,
And the one picture-book
Which makes us cry.
To open up means to die.

And the one picture of the summer house,
The house on Tarantula Rock,
The rocks forever losing as they live,
And in the living house, the jazz
Of Sarah Vaughn's incomprehensible good-byes
Drones on and on. And then the house is gone.

II

Thirty billion photographs,
Mr. Walker Evans said,
And only one or two important.
Only one or two.

Why important? Why praise?
Why now?
It is possible, Walker Evans said,
To kiss a shadow deep into the lips,
Because we ourselves are brilliant shadows.

III

Walker Evans evaporates out of the darkroom.
It is the terrible darkroom,
Where time is torn,
But only in the one overwhelming moment.
It is the uncertain darkroom,
Where the image of the body is always desiring,
And desire itself is homeless.
And to find the body means to lose it.

IV

And you too, stranger,
You also come from the darkroom.
You also pull the erotic black wing
Of the photograph
From the dark water,
To dry it out, to save it,
And give it back its flight.

This is how, at times, you fall asleep.
The flesh which harbors you
Falls asleep.
And your head drains out on the pillow,
And your black crow comes alive.

V

Down grinds the dirt, down rubs the bodies,
And Matthew Brady spoke of a hole so large —
In the heart, he said—
Larger than the bodies
Heaped up for burial,
Larger than the brevity of our lives.

And you, our lady of the spasm,
With your wet lunar nature and persistent hope,
You go to meet the skinny, bone-faced boys,
Down by a summer river,
Not far from the summer house,
And you try to fill the great hole in each.

VI

And after each repeated defeat,
When things mean so much more
As they fade,
You try again, you try again,
As when Matthew Brady's eye
Caught the young hipbones in moonlight,
As when Matthew Brady
Caught the uniform snow and your crows,
Falling on the dead soldier-boys.

This is how, at times,
Your head drains out on the pillow.
After the war, another war,
And the sheets are moist in the morning.

Afterword

These poems cling fiercely to their images. They are like a roomful of photographs. They are stubborn and don't want to be explained. They won't make themselves easier, no matter how many times we read them. Information and familiarity only sharpen and deepen their mystery.

The title, "The Lonesome Beauty of the Moment," is one of the ways of putting the meaning of the Japanese word *Yūgen*. Also "the beauty of mystery and depth," "the beauty of the deep, dark, and profound," and "the beauty not merely of appearances, but of the spirit, the difficult-to-see truth color of the universe."

These poems belong within the spirit of *Yūgen*, not within what has come to be the dominant spirit of contemporary American poetry, allegiant to narrative, sequential time and the singularity of personal experience, proud of its passage through time, proud of its sensibility, proud of the images it has trapped.

Yūgen is not much interested in the ego. The ego is merely the place where images happen. *Yūgen* always has the feeling-tone of universal sadness, because the truth of the universe always points toward an intense suffering as a result of being human.

These poems are concerned with the music they make. I don't mean just the rhythms and tonalities of the words, though that plays in. I'm talking about the music of the whole movement of idea/language/image, the way one saying flows out of another, or maybe snaps back at an angle, spirals, and then jumps ahead. They break from syntactic and narrative normalities, they make use of the absolute form of clauses, so that strings of images hang together primarily by proximity. Things not herded into place jump back and forth, rub, flash, change shape.

The earliest history of photography with its remarkable personalities strikes the poet's queer fascination and shatters into wild and disconnected facts. Linear time is then burnt from them, and they are recomoposed among the living chemicals in the darkroom.

It's a music possible only when linear time has been turned off. Then, when all the directions of expected discourse have stopped, the kind of pooling, reiterative, allusive motion begins, which is music, which is the photographic image emerging in the bath.

The images themselves are everything: the universe, the music, the striking particularity. In these poems they live their own intense life. At the same time the poems reveal themselves as deeply "personal," but not in that ego-centered modern way. The "I" that appears occasionally is itself only another image. The "personal" I'm talking about lies deeper than that. This is an aspect of *Yūgen*.

What I'm finally aware of is that everything—soldier, photographic plates, young Japanese monk, tarantula, moan of Billie Holiday, Daguerre's diorama in flames—is the self of the maker of the poems as he came on it in the process of saying the images, saying the poem. As independent as every moment is, nothing is random and apart. And the poem is about the dance of images, not about what an "I" thinks or feels or senses.

The images don't explain anything. They reveal themselves. They have powerful, coruscating, iridescent relationships. Things happen among the images. The whole has the immense clarity of a dream working itself out. But here the dreamer is awake. Or, we are enabled to share the mode of wakefulness of the dream fabricator.

Fire and photograph. War, woman, the one in the green dress. The one who falls asleep and her "black crow comes alive." The darkroom, the dark room. Grinding down and flaring up. And how well I know

> The sluggish heart of bear begins a dream in men
> Who also feel a passion for the light.

Like Eros, an image (a photograph) can represent both the danger and beauty of losing one's self. When images are intimate with both the dark and the light, they can contain a secret erotic grammar, capable of illuminating us or wounding us. And of course, some images are bigger than we are. They have the extreme power to surpass us and arouse us with a disturbance, a fluidic state which begins visually and then goes on to spread throughout our blood. Like a kiss, or a war-wound, stillness may be the first note of a music. We call this ecstasy.

An ecstasy, a paradise, "a garden inclosed." A camera is a box, and an image is always framed. Our heads and our bodies are also boxes, taking in the light of inspiration and the dark which can cripple. Beds and graves are paradise as well.

So the music spreads in ripples. What is so marvellous in these poems is that nothing *means* this or that. It all shines with great clarity. And vanishes again, and the vanishing hurts.

> *Their dirty faces, their ten thousand tiny jumping feet,*
> *All flame, all gone now, all gone, all black...*

Everything *refers*, round and round, and across. *That* is what I turn to poetry for.

It's absolutely a poem from psyche. There's no room for the defining, distancing intellect in this poem. It just gets confused. And time. Well, time here is photograph, grave, fireworks, soldier, desire. Body and image are as close as they can come, and the imaging psyche has its own intelligence, and a fierce, close understanding it is.

> *And after, like the migratory wings*
> *That swarmed in to eat the berry-tree,*
> *You moved on.*

An image can have the power of a living or dead person who is present. Timelessness and loss can be experienced simultaneously. You can carry a singular moment around with you, like a snapshot in your wallet. You can keep it in the secret dark of a drawer which is like a shrine.

And we are back to *Yūgen*.

— Cal Kinnear
Seattle, 1991